Living in Java under Japanese Occupation during World War Two

L. KOCH-LÜTHY
(1888 - 1975)

Contents

Foreword by Ysabelle Taylor

This is the account of my grandmother's experience of life in Java during the Second World War years. Her daughter Dikky, was my mother. I heard many stories about my mother's teenage life in Java when I was growing up, and in adulthood I came across the journal written by my grandmother. My understanding is that she was hoping it would be published. She wanted to bring to the attention of the world her experiences, and those of other foreigners living in Java at this time, which in 1960, when she finished writing this, was probably not well documented. As far as I know it was never published in any form, so now I am completing my grandmother's work for her. There are other accounts of lives in the Dutch East Indies during this period, but each person's experience is unique, and each gives a new perspective on the same events. So I believe it is important that this manuscript is available for anyone who is interested in it. She weaves her personal experiences into the historical context of events which makes a colourful and informative interpretation.

These are my grandmother's words. Occasionally they may not quite make sense, but I prefer to leave them to the interpretation of the reader than to impose my interpretation on them. My grandmother spoke English, French and Dutch, perhaps other languages, but I don't know for certain. She was born of Swiss parents who lived in England at the time of her birth. Her life up until the move to Java had been divided between England, France, Switzerland and Holland and this may explain her way of constructing sentences in English. She had been a nurse during the first World War.

Sadly, my grandmother was already suffering from dementia when I met her as a small child, but I remember a very dignified lady who was always smart and elegant. I called her "Granny Swiss" because she then lived in Switzerland. Her favourite phrase as we used to drive her out from her care home for tea was: "What a lot of cars!" What would she make of the world today! Her account describes the journey from Europe to Batavia (Jakarta in Java) by plane which, in 1940, took in the region of two weeks. She compares the changes twenty years later in 1960 when the same journey took "only" 36 hours.

According to my mother, my grandfather owned one plantation in Java and was a director in a company owning three more. Dutch white people managed and administered the plantations and managed the Javanese workers. When the story starts my grandmother and mother are living in Switzerland having separated from my grandfather, though not divorced. My grandmother was his second wife, his first wife having died and left him with a daughter. My mother's half sister was ten years older than her. She married a Dutchman which was the reason that she and her husband were put into Japanese camps. My grandparents and mother on the other hand held Swiss passports, and Switzerland was a neutral country during World War Two.

My mother, Dikky, did not experience the war in the same way as her mother, although she remembered the events. According to her accounts to me, she mostly remembered being a teenager who was in love with a Dutch boy living across the road who she met after the Japanese invasion. She mentioned in later life what a brave woman her mother had been to protect her from the horrors of the war as much as she could.

I am not a historian. I have attempted to keep dates and names accurate with research, but this is my grandmother's account, and so I take no responsibility for any mistakes in historical dates or facts.

There are very few family photographs from this time, but one of my grandmother and mother at the temple of Borobudur, when they were sighting seeing in time of peace before the war in Asia broke out, and a couple of their house in Bandung give a certain hint of the times. The travel documents show the routes travelled to and from Asia.

My grandmother's closing thoughts concerning the differences between people of varying cultures and attitudes around the globe, and her hope for them all to live in peace together without judgment resonates with the hopes of many today despite the sadly heart breaking conflicts which continue to blight the world.

Please note that some of the words, comments and phrases used by my grandmother are not politically correct in this day and age of 2019, as this document was written some 70 years ago.

Ysabelle Taylor 2019

Introduction

When, in December 1939, my husband and stepdaughter left together for Java, now named Indonesian Republic, and no longer a Dutch colony, war was imminent in Europe and we had the feeling of impending catastrophe all around. They had come from Holland, and on their way to Genoa where their ship left for Batavia, came to take leave of us. Our daughter "Dikky", who was then 12 years old, and I were staying in a little town on the lake of Geneva (Switzerland). My husband remarked: "you will probably be safer here than anywhere else, and we shall return from Java in May". He had to inspect four different plantations (quinine, coffee and rubber) belonging to a Dutch company, a trip he made every three or four years.

Winter came and went, and the air-mail arrived regularly from Java. At the beginning of May 1940, Holland was invaded by the German army. What would my husband do?

Then a few days later I received a cable from Cairo: "unable return Holland, taking same boat back to Java. Come with Dikky and join me there as soon as possible". He wrote a letter. They had heard of the invasion of Holland on the radio when the ship was in the Suez Canal. It was decided the ship would return at once to Java as most of the passengers were Dutch.

Three weeks of rush for Dikky and me.

I had to borrow money, get my Swiss passport seen to in Bern, vaccination, travelling agencies, packing etc. and I was lucky enough get the last two seats on what turned out to be the last KLM (Dutch) passengers' plane which left Naples two days before Italy came into the war. We took the Orient Express to Milan, then on to Naples.

Dikky had a high temperature and chickenpox of which there had been cases at her school. I showed the doctor at Naples a roll of bank notes. He wrote out a health certificate for the manager of the Hotel where we stayed three days, and another one for the agent of the KLM.... And he departed a richer man as there were twenty-two passengers instead of eleven, fortunately no other children. Two of the passengers were so ill, heart and lungs, they nearly died, and wherever we stopped a doctor came to attend to them. We went to Athens, Alexandria, Jerusalem, Bassora (Basrah, Iraq), Djask on the coast of Persia, Karachi, Jodhpur, Allahabad and Calcutta where there was the most awful storm I have ever

7

witnessed overnight. Then on to Rangoon, Bangkok, Penang, Singapore, Medan, Batavia and at last the airport of Bandung where my husband and step-daughter welcomed us.

The same now is done in practically 36 hours nonstop now!

Chapter 1
WAR

The Dutch Indies are situated, roughly speaking, between the Indian Ocean to the West and the Pacific Ocean to the East. Their nearest points of contact to the South are Australia, and to the North the Malay Peninsular, Indo-China and the Philippine Islands to which the American government had promised independence for 1945. This immense archipelago consists of about three thousand islands, the largest of which are Sumatra, Java, the greater part of Borneo, the whole of Celebes, and about half of New Guinea.

Everywhere the responsible, important and well remunerated posts were occupied by the Dutch and the Netherlands Indies was considered to be a model of colonisation. Many of the better class Indonesians had been to Europe or America, but, as everywhere else in Asia, the contact of old and sleeping civilisations with the Occidental dynamism gradually awakened unexpected reactions and gave birth to Asiatic nationalism.

The "Malays", who inhabit the greater part of Indonesia, have received their culture from India and, except for a few minorities, their religion is Islam. The majority have for three centuries been under Dutch administration, but their nationalities look to India as an example and leader.

"The evolution of every colonial country is governed by certain common fundamentals which neither race nor culture, not colonial policy can alter - fundamentals which are indeed the very fruit of that policy. For it is the impact of the West, of its intellectual and dynamic qualities on the sleeping civilisations of the East, that has grown to colonial nationalism in its very existence and its incentive. And it is more especially Western eduction that has provided it with its ideals and with its weapons.".

On the 7th December 1941, totally unexpectedly, and without warning, the Japanese Air Force bombed and destroyed American battleships at Pearl Harbour, Hawaii. The United States, Great Britain and Holland were at war with Japan. By declaring war immediately, Holland, in all probability, saved Australia, as the Japanese were forced for strategic reasons to fight the Dutch Indies first and leave enormous occupation forces there.

Then began for us a time feverish activity and preparation.

Japanese shops were closed down and all Japanese arrested. Red Cross posts were organised, public and private air raid shelters built, sirens for air raid warnings established at different points of the town, orders for total black-out were given and dark blue curtains were put at the windows as soon it became dark. First aid classes were formed, lectures and demonstrations given by doctors and nurses. Gas masks were issued and I remember seeing my husband prancing around in a silk Japanese dressing gown with his gas mask on, a grotesque figure. All the Dutch land, sea and air forces were mobilised.

My step-daughter arrived with her husband from Buitenzorg (a hill station in Java) with their luggage, and hoped their furniture would follow. My son-in-law enlisted as a soldier and, after being trained, served an anti-aircraft battery on the flying field and had one or two narrow escapes. As I had a nurse's certificate and had nursed during the first world war in both France and England, I was asked to assist the resident's wife at the nearest Red Cross post. Dikky learnt bandaging and first aid and my step-daughter worked at the Red Cross offices in town.

Some Europeans left with their families by air for Australia, but my husband, who loved his plantation, would not hear of deserting his work and the people who were dependent on him. So we all stayed together to face what might come.

We listened to the radio; surely America and Great Britain would help us.

Lord Wavell arrived with a small British Force, to cooperate with the Dutch.

The Japanese advanced.

The Philippines were taken.

One island after another was invaded. Singapore, the gateway of the East was attacked by sea, by land and from the air and forced to capitulate in February 1942. The English had believed it to be impregnable … The Dutch were outnumbered by ten to one, it would be impossible for them to resist for any length of time. I remember our feelings when Wavell arrived … in the nick of time!

The Japanese were slowly but surely closing in on us and Java would be the last of the Islands to be attacked. Their planes began to circle above Bandung. One tried to do one's shopping before the hours when we knew they could be expected over the town. Bombs were dropped on the airfield, quinine factory, post office, on roads and houses and on native villages. I had bought stamps in the post office ten minutes before a bomb fell in front of it, killing a number of people whose remains were picked off bicycles left outside. Another bomb fell on a shop I had also been in the same morning… just luck.

We had a good air raid shelter in the back garden made of hard quinine wood from the plantation, and partly underground. There was room for about twenty people. I put in tins of food, drinking water, first aid kit, rugs and pillows. We were thankful to have one shelter when the actual fighting was only a few miles away distance, and bombs were dropping all around. Sometimes, when we were having our meals, which was most annoying, the servants, excepting the cook who always stayed to help, were frightened and used to run home to their families in the kampong near by. The baby of our head boy was born during an air raid. Once a British staff officer came to our shelter. His native chauffeur had refused to drive any further…

Neighbours who had no shelters, came to ours, and once an exhausted Dutch sergeant tumbled in. He had eaten nothing since two days after a bomb had exploded amongst them. He was trembling like a leaf, praying without ceasing, and half out of his mind. Between two air raids I ran into the pantry and heated a plateful of soup for him. Our dog, who also of course ran into the shelter with us was always very excited, but not in the least frightened. When the daughters were not at home, I was anxious and wondered where they could be sheltering. Once on their way back from town, a bomb exploded just opposite the shelter they happened to be in. After this experience they decided to remain at home.

We sent Dikky to stay with friends on a tea plantation thinking she would be safer there than in town. I gave her my wedding ring to wear on a gold chain around her neck and a list of friends and relatives in Europe who would eventually look after her if anything happened to her parents. But after ten days she begged to return to us, declaring she could not bear seeing the planes flying overhead to bomb Bandung and not know if we were still alive. Better to be blown out of existence together. So I went up to the plantation and fetched her back again.

There was an anti aircraft gun next to our garden, hidden amongst trees. If the Japs had located it, we wouldn't have stood a chance… The hospitals were filing up with the wounded, most of whom had never even seen a Japanese.

The Dutch were in no position really to wage war, still less were they able to resist the huge and highly mechanised modern Japanese army. The Dutch navy fought until most of their ships were sunk. I believe only one escaped. The airforce put up a brave show with antiquated planes. "Just suicide" the English said, when they saw them. The will to resist was there, but not the power. The anti-aircraft batteries on the Bandung airfield were not mobile and could not be rapidly moved from one spot to another. They were soon destroyed. Japanese pilots were

11

clever and audacious. They did some extraordinary "stunting" to entertain us. Once we witnessed a collision between two of their fighting planes, both came down, burning bits falling in every direction. The most I ever saw above the town were twenty-seven planes. In those days raids were not yet being made by several thousands. They flew in impeccable formation dropping bombs which looked like cloud puffs in the blue sky. They used only small bombs about 50 kilos, which individually did not great damage. A few houses and buildings collapsed, windows were smashed and pot holes made in the roads. No incendiary bombs were used... yet...

Further down the street we lived in, a bomb went through the roof of the house and exploded in the bedroom. Fortunately the old couple living there were already having breakfast in the room next door and crouched under the bomb proof dining room table. They were scared out of their wits, but unhurt. The bedroom was in a peaceful mess, the roof partly blown off, all the windows smashed (the neighbour's also) and part of the garden ploughed up. The old man was dazed and his wife weeping, but they refused to leave their house.

The army weak, demoralised, insufficiently trained and armed, capitulated on 7th March 1942, three months after having declared war on Japan. In Java the fighting only lasted a short while. There had been dreadful fighting up in the hills only a few miles from Bandung. The wounded were being brought down to the hospitals in trucks dripping with blood. The natives were fleeing towards the town. The Dutch didn't stand a chance and were simply being machine gunned by low flying Japanese planes. Ghastly tales were being circulated about the methods used by the Japs to dispatch their prisoners (they had not signed the Geneva Red Cross Convention) and how starving Kampong dogs, attracted by the smell, tore the corpses to pieces.

The day before the capitulation the Japanese gave us a demonstration with thirty planes of what they could do in the way of destruction and had warned headquarters that unless their terms of unconditional surrender were accepted the following day (Sunday) the town would be wiped out within half and hour. I thought Saturday night might be our last on earth ...

Thank God they did capitulate, for it would only have been useless slaughter to continue to resist. We heard the news of the capitulation on the radio, whilst outside on the road in the sunshine the first shock troops were already passing in trucks; a horrible lot of bestial, brutal looking men, armed to the teeth. One felt sick.

The Japanese army tramped during several days into town. As our house was situated on one of the principal roads leading to it, we watched from behind the curtains. The soldiers had a curious shuffling gait, their uniforms were kaki-grey-green and many of them wore black cloth boots with a separate big toe and rubber soles. They were small, had bandy legs and straight black hair cut very short. Most of them wore spectacles and nearly all had gold fillings in their teeth. We learnt to loathe the sight of their gleaming hypocritical smiles, their sly slanting eyes.

The inhabitants had been warned by the Dutch authorities not to have any alcohol in their houses. Consequently, before the arrival of the Japanese troops, we spent a good hour emptying whisky, wine and liqueurs down the sink and then tossed the empty bottles over the back garden wall. The Japanese had requested the Dutch to evacuate the schools and a certain number of public buildings. For some reason (perhaps lack of organisation and time) this had not been done. Therefore, during more than a week the troops simply installed themselves in private houses. Their occupants had to ask for shelter in those that were not occupied by the Japanese. As we had a Swiss emblem on our front door we were not thrown out and given permission to remain where we were.

One wet day, about twenty Japanese soldiers and an officer walked in. They had on muddy boots, looked around and asked if they might boil their rice, and bathe in the servant's quarter. The officer spoke a little English. We offered them tea and were told there was no longer any sugar in Tokyo. Some of them were wounded and I changed their soiled bandages. By the time they left again my white drawing room carpet was ruined.

Chapter 2
During the Japanese Occupation:
Inside and outside the camps

At the beginning of the Japanese occupation, life went on much as usual for civilians, who were certainly far from realising what the future held in store for them. The Japanese authorities began by putting all the Dutch prisoners of war into camps. At first they were permitted to receive the visits of near relatives, even friends, who brought them money, clothes and food. Later on they were entirely isolated and it was not possible to communicate in any way with them. The Dutch Governor General A.W.L. Tjarda van Starkenborgh Stachouwer (whose wife was American) and most of the high officials were arrested and disappeared, no-one knew where to. Eventually after the Japanese capitulation they were discovered by the Allies in Moukden (China).

,The civilians, who on the arrival of the Japanese had been forced to leave their homes, were able at last to return to them and found them in a dreadful condition; curtains and clothes stolen or simply cut to shreds, food thrown about, beds soiled, linen torn, silver taken, furniture destroyed and gardens dug up in the search of arms, jewellery or money. Everything was indescribably filthy. They had ruined all they could.

When I went to see my Red Cross post I sat down and wept. It took three of us about five hours to try to clean up the mess. The clean dressings and bandages were torn and soiled, contents of tubes squeezed out on the walls, pots and medicine bottles smashed, extra linen and clothing gone. The soldiers had evidently had a glorious time and done the job thoroughly.

Every European had to report himself to the Japanese authorities, was questioned and given (for a big sum) a special identification card complete with photograph and thumb print (see photo page 38). Neutral had to wear special badges. In front of the town hall public bonfires were made of Dutch flags, portraits of the Dutch Royal family and Dutch school books which the Dutch authorities as well as the schools and populations, were compelled to witness.

Gradually Japanese officials and civilians arrived from Japan to take over all the posts occupied by the Dutch who were then dismissed and interned. As long as a Dutchman was needed by the Japs, in the posi-

14

tion he held, he was allowed to return home or remain in a "family camp" with his wife and children.

Shortly after the Dutch Indies had declared war on Japan most of the Germans living in the Indies who the Dutch had interned were sent by the Dutch authorities in three ships to the British India "out of harm's way". Two of these ships were torpedoed (a Japanese "mistake") and 400 Germans were sent to the bottom of the sea. The occupants of the third ship remained during, and after the war, in a camp in British India. Only two years after the Japanese capitulation were German women and children sent to the isle of "Ournst" to await transportation to Europe. One of my friends, a charming Viennese woman, died there.

Shortly after Bandung was occupied, my husband decided to let our house to some French people and we went up to the quinine plantation above Bandung. When we arrived there all Europeans, excepting the younger men who had been called up to join the army, were still on the plantation with their families and work was going on as usual. Gradually however, conditions changed for the worse.

One never knew who would be interned next. The natives began to be restless and disagreeable, food was difficult to procure, medical supplies for the dispensary equally so, and radio forbidden. We had more and more the feeling of being spied on by our servants. The manager was called up several times by the Japanese before being finally interned. He was only allowed to take a few clothes with him in a small handbag. A native manager was put in his place. Native police patrolled the grounds to prevent the looting of houses which Europeans had been forced to leave. A Japanese officer arrived one day, and nearly discovered the radio which my step-daughter had in one of her trunks, after which we spent three horrible nights destroying the thing, burning the parts that could be burnt, and either burying or sinking in the pond the metal parts we could not destroy.

No-one ventured any more far from the house.

One night we had an earthquake. I woke up feeling bewildered and giddy. The whole house was rocking. Ceilings came down and cupboards were overturned. The walls were cracking. I managed to get in the next room and pull the manager's mother in law, an old lady over seventy, out of bed. She just escaped being killed by a block of stone that fell on her pillow. Fortunately no-one was hurt. Dikky was staying with some people we knew and slept through it all; unbelievable!

House keeping became more and more of a problem and soon we were the only white people left. Japanese came up to see the plantation and to be entertained by my husband and shown over the grounds and factory. After several more weeks, during which the former manager's wife and family were fetched by the police to be interned (the mother died in a camp), and never knowing what the following day would bring us, we persuaded my husband to leave the plantation before being told to quit by the Japanese. We returned to Bandung after an absence of eight months to find those of our friends who were not neutrals already in camps. Now and again were received news secretly, but it was dangerous.

Finally, my step-daughter who had no idea what had happened to her Dutch husband after he had been transferred from his camp in town, was also taken to be interned. The Japanese system was always to "save face" and "turn the screw" little by little. For some time we were able to communicate with her, and even see her. She was allowed to take with her, anything and everything she wished - even a dog - and settled down comfortably in the part of town where a number of houses had been wired off. Women who were friends could arrange to live together with their children and take servants with them. There was a market in the camp and food shops, a hospital and classes for the children. People remaining outside the camp, mostly Eurasians and neutrals, gave them silver and jewels to be kept by those in the "protection camps" (as the Japanese insisted they should be called) and I remember wishing I could be "protected" too!

However, as the camp filled up, gradually space grew less and food scarce. Market and shops were abolished, furniture was thrown out to make more room, bicycles, refrigerators and sewing machines simply "taken away". We heard nothing more and could no longer smuggle food or letters to the unfortunate inmates. Only after the capitulation of the Japanese in August 1945 did we get to know of all that happened, and how finally they were half starved, lying on dirty mattresses on the floor, packed like sardines. The awful heat, mosquitoes, flies and bugs. No soap, promiscuity, illness and epidemics. The Japs tried to break their spirits (and backs) by forcing them to work in quarries or dig ground. The guards looked on, laughing, and any lack of discipline was punished by thrashing or having to stand in the blazing sun. Everything depended on the Japanese at the head of the camps, and most of them were brutes.

The cemetery, outside Bandung, where those who died in camps were buried, grew larger and larger. In one of the worst camps, dogs and monkeys were trained to bite the inmates, and those who tried to escape from the camp were liable to be shot down. The prisons were also full, only sitting or standing room, filthy conditions, people half naked in rags they wore for months, starving … glad to die …

Two or three times whole camps were made to move to other places to prevents plots or "listening in". Each time there was a move, conditions became worse and possessions had to be left behind until finally some had nothing left but the clothes they stood up in. Any human Japanese who showed pity or offered help, was dismissed and replaced by another who knew better how to handle those under his care.

But, to give the devil his due, I know personally of some cases where Europeans owed their lives to Japanese who had some pity in their hearts. The Japanese who were utterly unburdened by scruples, were, as a rule, kind to children and apparently loved flowers. They were extremely frugal and their armies were supplied with rice, dried vegetables and fish and vitamin pills; a distinct advantage over the allied armies who had to be followed up by tons of canned food. The Japanese fought well, and were physically fit, well trained and excellent soldiers. To make the supreme sacrifice for their emperor was the highest ambition of every Japanese and they were frightened of nothing. After the Japanese capitulation, a number of higher officers committed hara-kiri rather than be taken prisoners by the "foreign devils". In occupied Java the discipline was good and, on the whole, the officers had the occupation troops well in hand, although sometimes they raided the kampongs for native women. Any thieving or pillaging by Chinese natives or their own men was swiftly and mercilessly punished.

The camps for the men were in some ways better as there were no small children. After the money the men had on entering the camps had gradually been spent on food smuggled in by the natives at black market prices, they too were reduced to semi-starvation. They bartered their clothes and finally sold the gold fillings in their teeth to obtain a little extra food or some cigarettes. When internees, for some reason or other, were sentenced to flogging or torture, the whole camp was forced to witness the proceedings. They were bullied, humiliated and treated like dogs. Working squads were sent to work in Bandung and had to walk for miles and miles on empty stomachs. They cultivated ground, built defences, felled trees etc. Many of them had to walk bare foot having no shoes any more to wear. We were sometimes allowed to pass them food and cigarettes, but talking was of course forbidden.

The Japanese indulged in neither gas chambers nor mass exterminations, but they employed other methods, such as sending thousands of prisoners of war to work on the celebrated Burma Railway, when most of them died of sunstroke and exhaustion. Very few survived. Others were exported to working camps in Siam and others, amongst whom my son in law, were taken to camps in Japan and put to work in copper mines etc.

17

Old men (civilians), from 60 - 70 years old, were transported in cattle truck on the railway from one part of Java to another. They stood for long hours with no shade, water or food. Those who died on the way were thrown out, the others after arrival didn't live long. Prisoners of war were permitted to send an official and censored post card once a year to say they were alive and well. Many of those in camps were so changed in appearance after three years as to be absolutely unrecognisable. Wives no longer knew their husbands, nor husbands their wives.

Perhaps one of the most cruel forms of moral torture the Japanese thought of was the sending to prisoner's wives of absolutely untrue reports of the death of men in the camps. Can one imagine anything more absolutely fiendish?

Chapter 3
Outside the camps

At first conditions were not so bad as might have been expected. As all motor cars were requisitioned by the Japanese military authorities, most people, including ourselves, took to cycling and bought bicycles. Fortunately both my husband and I had cycled in our youth. Dikky had learnt to cycle almost as soon as she could walk and my step-daughter took great trouble to learn. Neutrals had been told they might keep their cars by paying a big sum of money, which my husband considered worth while. Shortly afterwards there was no petrol to be had. This is an illuminating example of Japanese trickery. They were always delight to get the better of a European.

The rapid defeat of the Dutch in 1942 opened the eyes of the Indonesians to the intrinsic weakness of Dutch rule and paved the way for the success of a violent and extremely clever anti-white, particularly anti-Dutch propaganda, which the Japanese carried out on a grand scale during the three and a half years they occupied the islands. Although the Japanese were cordially hated for their oppression, the instrument was nevertheless prepared, ready for use against the Dutch when oppression would no longer be possible. Not only did the natives realise that the Dutch army, in which they had had utter confidence, had failed to protect them, but they witnessed now their humiliation and after having lost faith in the Dutch, lost all respect for them too.

Millions of natives welcomed the Japanese army by flag wagging the "rising sun"; little flags that had already been prepared in unlimited quantities in Tokyo. They drank in the diabolical propaganda. Propaganda inspired by the Nazis and adapted to Japanese aims. It was diffused by loud speakers at meetings, by newspapers published in Japanese native languages and in the native schools where Japanese was also taught. The result was a ferocious hatred against the white race. A police corps of more than 500,000 natives was created and worked under the orders of the "Kempeitai" - the Japanese Gestapo - some 200,000 natives were in enrolled in the Japanese army. The Japanese proved themselves past masters in the art of inoculating hate and evil and, through the methods they employed, turned a docile disciplined people into madmen out to kill.

I have watched bayonet practise on stuffed dummies ... and shuddered... I have seen Japanese soldiers demonstrate an attack, crawling on their bellies in the grass, so well camouflaged they were not to be distinguished at a distance. From the ground they advanced on, then at a

19

word of command, I have seen them leaping up brandishing their knives and emitting the most blood curdling yells, like wild beasts. The effect was sickening.

Not only were we obliged to bow low to the Japanese sentries who represented the Emperor, His Imperial Majesty Hirohito, but what was far worse, we had to incline ourselves also in front of native guards. If one forgot to do so, one was stopped and received a resounding smack in the face to remind one for next time. I cycled home a round about way to avoid passing them. Dikky was once hauled off her bicycle because she wore red, white and blue sandals. My husband returned home one day with his mouth bleeding, and I was knocked nearly senseless. People in the streets took no notice when such things happened; they could do nothing.

After a while Dutch schools, churches, banks and most shops were closed down and Japanese currency instituted. On the streets and in the shops (before these were closed) only Malay was allowed to be spoken. Neutrals who had bank accounts were allowed a small sum each month, quite insufficient to live on in the long run when prices went up sky high.

"Razzias" took place with the aid of native police who went from house to house looking for people in hiding, or hoping to discover hidden arms. Men, women and children were arrested without warning in the streets and driven away in trucks. One was constantly asked to produce one's identity and show one's neutral badge. Families never knew which of their members would be missing by the end of the day, nor where they had been taken to. People were dragged out of their beds or baths and sent with next to nothing on to prisons and camps.

The so-called "Blanda-Indos" or Eurasians were arrested if they couldn't prove they had a certain percentage of native blood. A neighbour of ours was marched off to the worst prison in Bandung and kept there a week until, thanks to a friend of his who knew an influential Jap in a high position, he was allowed to return home. He was weak and ill, on the verge of nervous breakdown, and had already caught dysentery and, of course, bugs. He told us he had been in a one man cell with eight others, most of them ill. The prison was over crowded, and dead were being buried at the rate of seven a day.

Another Dutchman we knew, a tea planter, had taken into his house for the night (after having obtained permission by telephone from the native authorities) two men and one woman. A dangerous thing to do, not knowing who they were, but they were Europeans. It was pouring and they were wet through. A few days later he was taken by the Japanese to

20

the "Kempei" and questioned. As he knew nothing about the people staying with him, it was impossible for him to answer. He was tortured regularly during twelve days, but could give no information on their whereabouts. Finally he was sent home a broken man, both physically and morally, with his two arms and hands quite useless.

The news of house searches went round like wildfire. One destroyed any compromising papers one might still have and threw a few necessary articles of clothing into a bag, and then ran to warn one's neighbour. Whilst the Japanese searched the house for a radio, one woman I knew staged a fainting fit in an armchair in the seat of which it was concealed. The clever Japs disdainfully ignored her and when they left again, having discovered nothing, she was still "unconscious"!

Telephones were removed, everything made of iron or metal was taken, such as fences, gates, lavatory fittings, bedsteads, pots and pans etc. Nothing was repaired any longer and whole houses were demolished by the Japanese for building purposes elsewhere. Roads became difficult to cycle on, and gardens and walkways overgrown with weeds. When rain came in through the roof, beds had to be moved around to keep dry. Refuse was no longer removed and had to be buried or burnt in the garden. Food began to be scarce.

Rice was rationed and sold secretly at black market prices. The natives were beginning to starve and could no longer cultivate their fields and gardens to feed their families. Their enthusiasm for the Japanese died down and turned to silent hate. One stayed at home as much as possible or sat in the garden behind the house where one could not be seen from the street.

All Dutch doctors had been interned by the Japanese, and the few doctors who were left to attend civilians were either neutral, Chinese or Eurasian. The nurses from the hospitals were also in camps and ignorant Eurasians and natives with no proper training were left to nurse the patients. Medicines and remedies were taken by the Japanese for their own hospitals where there were Japanese doctors, surgeons and nurses, all efficient and highly trained, but who refused to attend to Europeans. In the only hospital Europeans were accepted, everything was lacking, remedies, linen and food. One had to bring one's own linen and food and trust to luck that no-one stole it! As soon as possible the patients were sent home again.

When anyone died in Java, the corpse had to be buried within twelve hours on account of the climate. When, during the occupation, there were no coffins left, native mats were used. The natives always buried their dead in special sheets. As these were no longer obtainable they stole our sheets whenever possible. Poor Dikky was in hospital for her birthday two years running. The first time her appendix was removed by a Chinese surgeon. The second she very nearly died of dypyheria and was attended to by a Hungarian doctor. Before she had fully recovered her father had a bad accident. A passing truck threw him off his bicycle. He was picked up and taken unconscious to a Chinese surgeon who sewed up his leg. I had been telephoned for and we had to wait six hours in a garage until the only ambulance there was came and took him to the hospital where he remained three weeks. He was terribly bruised all over and in bad pain but fortunately, no bones broken. I was able to find two good nurses for day and night and I bought extra sheets, food and medicine for him. Troubles never seemed to end for I too fell off my bicycle and cut my chin open. A German surgeon sewed it up.

Prices began to soar fantastically. The Swiss, when their bank accounts were through, were able to borrow money from the Swiss consulate. Other people were helped along by wealthy Chinese. It was a dreadful time and no-one knew how long it would still last.

I gave English and French conversation lessons to be able to buy extra food and pay for my daughter's education - such as it was. My pupils were of every nationality, excepting Dutch.

The lowest class natives, and a great many Eurasians too, were starving and without clothes, so they took to stealing everything they could lay their hands on, anything they could eat, wear or sell. Poverty and lack of food make human being desperate. The servants of course lent a hand and had their share of the spoils, but one could prove nothing. I sold my evening clothes to Eurasians who did business with the Japanese and my husband some European suits, which, we were told, were exported to Japan. We bartered or sold curtains, bedspreads, sheets, towels, table cloths, in fact any material we had to obtain food and money. Better that than wait until they were stolen!

One night I was awakened by the noise of smashing glass. By the time I was out of bed and in the room next to mine, the window curtains had been torn down and the thieves disappeared into the night with their booty. We had engaged a native night watchman but when he slept behind the house, they stole in front, and vice versa. Another time the exterior window tents were cut away and electric light bulbs had gone too. I suspect the night watchman was in the know and got his percentage!

Three of the thieves were eventually caught. We were not the only victims, they even dared to break into houses the Japanese were living in. Strangely enough most of the watch dogs had died in a mysterious way. The three ragged natives were tried and proved guilty and as my

22

husband was not yet well enough to cycle to town, I had to go to court. The Indonesian judge asked me some questions in Malay which, without thinking, I answered in French. The conversation then continued between us fluent in French and I heard later that he had studied Law in Paris! The three wretched culprits stood up to hear the verdict and were condemned to one year's imprisonment. This meant almost certain starvation as criminals were fed only on "oubis" a kind of native potato which had next to no nutritional qualities. I felt quite sorry for them, especially the the oldest made and deep bow and humbly thanked the judge.

Chapter 4
News of the Capitulation of Germany - the bombing of Hiroshima and Nagasaki and the capitulation of Japan

News tricked through, and in the camps, under the very noses of the Japanese guards and spies, secret radios were listened to. News spread from mouth to mouth, but no sign was ever given that we all knew, more or less, what was happening in Europe. There were several false alarms that Germany had capitulated. We knew that Italy had changed sides, because the Italians in Bandung were rounded up, requested to leave their homes and obliged to go and live, under control, in one of the hotels in the town.

After June 22nd 1941 we also knew of the German armies rapid advance in Russia and it was touch and go that the Russians in the vicinity were not also put in camps. They were however left in peace. Perhaps the Japanese thought this the best policy for the time being. During six months the Russians fought a defensive war, then when in December 1941, Moscow was about to fall, the tide turned in favour of the Russians who ended up completely beating the German forces and whose army was eventually the first to enter Berlin.

Already in 1943 we knew the allies were preparing to invade Germany, probably from the Western side. For a year we hoped and prayed for its success knowing what a colossal undertaking it would be and how long it would take to prepare every detail. It had to succeed, and it would succeed. We lived on that hope.

Then at last news of the invasion of the allied armies on the coast of Normandy on June 6th 1944. The Japanese admitted it about two weeks later in the local paper.

Between the allied armies to the West and South, and the Russians to the East, the Germans were forced to evacuate the countries they had invaded and occupied since four long years, and were eventually to submit to unconditional surrender after the capture of Berlin on May 7th 1945. The fall of Germany was told to my husband by a neighbour who crept up to his window during the night. There had been already so many rumours that, when it was actually true, no-one could believe it. The Japanese, as usual, postponed printing the news as long as possible.

This victory however, did not alleviate any of our actual troubles, but the knowledge that Europe was at last free of the Nazi yoke kept up our spirits. For all of us, and the starving inmates of the camps, the question now was, "how long would it take to make the Japanese capitulate? What were the allied plans in the Far East, would any of us still be alive to tell the tale?"

One had the feeling worse was to come …

Hiroshima was bombed with one atomic bomb by the Americans on August 6th 1945.

Nagasaki on August 9th with another.

Hiroshima, the headquarters of the Japanese army defending Southern Japan, was a major military storage and assembly point. Nagasaki was a major sea port containing several industrial plants of great wartime importance.

The offer to surrender, after a prolonged Japanese cabinet session in which His Majesty Hirohito, Emperor of Japan intervened, was made on August 15th. The allied terms were unconditional surrender with a reservation concerning the sovereignty of the Emperor. The Emperor of Japan was, before the present attempt of the American army to turn Japan into a democratic state, considered by his 78,000,000 subjects to be a God. Not only was he the head of the state, he WAS the state, and Japan was ruled in his name. He lived in the hidden, inner halls of Kyajo Palace in the centre of Tokyo surrounded by a tremendous granite wall some miles in length. Every precaution was taken to guard him and, when he left the Palace, streets were shut off and every building on the route rigidly inspected. No-one might look at the Emperor, people had to turn their backs on him when he passed and he was never referred to by name, but called "Son of Heaven" or "Sublime Majesty". He was born in Tokyo in 1901 and, when on Christmas Day 1926 he ascended the throne, he became the 124th Emperor of Japan in an unbroken dynasty. He was educated by tutors in the Peer's School and went abroad on a trip to Europe. The present Emperor's grand father, Mutsuhito, who reigned from 1868 - 1911, was during 44 years one of the greatest rulers in Asia. But the foundation of the dynasty dates back over 2000 years to 660 B.C. to the first Emperor Jimmu who was a fifth generation descendant of the Sun Goddess, the chief Japanese Deity. The dynasty never died out nor was it overthrown. The Japanese are naturally fertile and in Japan adoption of a son is the legal equivalent to actually kinship. Also, in the old days, Japanese Emperors were not monogamous.

Shintoism is the national religion and is a combination of Ancestor worship and patriotism. All Japanese have a common descent from the Sun Goddess (they don't allow you to forget it either) and all consider themselves to be members of the same great family with the Emperor at its head.

Hirohito is sportive, but very short sighted and, like so many of his subjects, wears spectacles. It is said he never wears any clothes twice, not even underwear, and his chief hobbies are supposed to be marine biology and photography. His marriage to beautiful Princess Nagako was a love match and arranged in spite of serious opposition. His bride was not directly a member of the great Fujiwara family which, by tradition 1300 years old, was the sole family group from which Empresses might be chosen. Six children have been born, first four daughters. The Crown Prince Akihito was born in 1933.

The two atomic bombs put a sudden unforeseen and unexpected - unhoped for, I should say - end to the Japanese war. They brought death to over 100,000 Japanese, but rendered unnecessary the incendiary raids, the strangling blockade and the American invasion planned for November 1st to begin with the Southern Island of Kyushu. The war might have continued another year or more, with huge losses on both sides and, before the end, probably every European in the Dutch East Indies, as in other parts of Asia occupied by the Japanese, would all have been wilfully massacred, including men, women and children in civilian camps, all prisoners of war and the neutrals who were still free.

The Japanese government had received due warning, we were afterwards to learn, from the United States and the Chinese government in the Potsdam ultimatum of July 26th. It was disdainfully rejected by Premier Suzuki on July 28th. The ultimatum promised the destruction of Japan if resisted, without actually mentioning the atomic bomb about which absolute secrecy was kept until the New Mexico test on July 16th. The Japanese forces numbered over 5,000,000 men. The two atomic bombs cost the lives of 100,000 Japanese citizens. It was the only issue to end the war in the Pacific.

The news of the Japanese capitulation seemed too good to be true, and we were fairly stunned by the unexpectedness of it. Curiously enough, we expected the American army to come and relieve us of the Japanese occupation forces and scanned the skies, hopefully waiting and watching for American planes to drop pamphlets, if not parachutists.

We waited in vain and were informed that, for the time being, we had been put by the allies under Japanese "Protection" and that they were to be held responsible for our lives and welfare! Strange turn of events indeed …

Their "protection" proved, nevertheless to be efficacious and one has to grudgingly admit that, until the arrival of the British Indian troops, their protection was efficient and thorough. Although they proceeded to protect the Europeans with one hand and deal out arms with the other to the natives.

Almost immediately after capitulation, the Japs played their last trump card and proclaimed on 17th August at Batavia (Djakarta), the foundation of the Indonesian Republic! The republican flags replaced those of the rising sun.

Chapter 5
Arrival of British troops and the native revolt and uprising.

Little by little the civilian camps were opened and their occupants permitted out on parole at fixed hours.

We received news from my step-daughter from a camp she had been removed to near Batavia. I shall never forget my three hours bicycle ride on impossible pot holed roads to the nearest men's camp to bring food to various friends there. We were laughing and crying together; so much to tell, to hear and to ask about. Only when the camps were opened and families and friends reunited, did one realise how many were missing. Those who could prove they had a place to live in, or friends to receive them, were permitted to depart, but many alas returned to their camps, finding more food provided for them there since the capitulation than what the friends who had not been interned had managed to collect and save in their larders. During two weeks we had ten people in our house, sleeping on improvised mattresses and who had to be fed and cared for. Their joy at being free at last, at having a bath, clean clothes and mattresses, sufficient food, made us realise, more than ever, how fortunate had been those the right side of the hated wire. We felt ashamed of being still as comfortable as before.

One old friend remained three months with us, having nowhere else to go until he could get to his sugar plantation the other end of Java, and our garage was turned into a bedroom for sundry people, the car having long since been taken by the Japanese.

The unexpected surrender of the "yellow brothers" had taken the allies by surprise and it was only at the beginning of September the British troops were able to enter Singapore. On September 29th, after six endless weeks of Japanese protection, the first contingent of British Indian Gurkha troops from Burma where they had been fighting, commanded by their British officers, arrived in Batavia (Java), in so few numbers as to be only able, at first, to hold small areas: the cities of Surabaya, Semarang, and corridor from two to six miles wide connecting and including Batavia and Bandung. These six weeks were put to good use by the natives, who, encouraged of course by the Japanese authorities, and quite against allied orders, took over all public services ... even the police! Soekarno, the so called president of the Indonesian Republic had a free hand.

28

This Indonesian leader began life humbly in Surabaya and is today a good looking man of forty-six. He has a large following of fanatical Indonesian admirers and is a good orator with the power to fascinate and hold his native audience. Soekarno is his christian name, a common one in Java. Javanese are somewhat careless about surnames. He studied architecture and engineering, but ended up by taking politics up as an occupation. By his present wife, whom he married because his first wife bore him no children, he has a young son. Native unrest had been stirring for year and when, in 1926, the Dutch, in suppressing a communist uprising, exiled some 4500 Indonesians to New Guinea, Soekarno became an uncompromising but non-communist nationalist, and was exiled to Flores Island in 1934. He was still there when the Dutch East Indies were attacked by the Japanese. His resolutely pro-Japanese attitude won for him a decoration and ample funds.

When, two days after the capitulation of the Japanese, as a parting gift to the Indonesians and parting shot to the Dutch, they proclaimed the foundation of the Indonesian Republic and they offered the presidency to Soekarno. He lives in the fine mansion that once belonged to the Dutch Resident, situated in Central Java near Borobudur, the massive and imposing Buddhist Temple where Java's kings worshipped eight centuries before the Dutch came to the archipelago.

Thanks to clever propaganda, Australian and American sympathy was won for the Indonesian cause and the British General Christison announced he would hold the republic responsible (this time!) for the safety of all Europeans in the part of the Dutch East Indies they (the republicans) occupied as the British troops were not in sufficient numbers to spread over the whole of Java. The Japanese continued secretly passing their arms to the natives, and organised their resistance.

The Native Uprising

In October the real trouble began and, for some weeks, we lived in daily terror of having to flee from our home, of kidnapping, shooting and street fighting. The natives put up barricades and thousands of them assembled on the outskirts of town. Hundreds of Dutch were massacred but only after two British high officers were killed by the natives did the British occupation troops receive orders to adopt a firmer attitude and take reprisals.

Lieutenant Governor General Hubertus van Mook, born in Java of Dutch parentage, Minister of the Dutch Colonies from 1942-1945 for the exiled government in London, endeavoured to restore order and attempted to negotiate with the Indonesians, but in vain. The British who had received orders to protect the Dutch, liberate those who were interned and disarm the Japanese, were in a difficult position. An officer once said to me "We are here to protect the Europeans, but not to fight the natives" to which I replied "Well, I expect you will discover you won't be able to do the one without the other."

All British troops and British-Indian troops in the tropics wore uniforms of "jungle green". In fact, everything they wore and used was of this colour, including underclothes, towels, socks, handkerchiefs, mosquito nets, the tin cans containing army rations and the silk used for parachutes. Even the toilet paper was jungle green! Everything and everybody was camouflaged to seem to melt into their surroundings. The Gurkhas were olive skinned little fellows, strong as tigers, and with the Sikhs, said to be the best fighters and soldiers on earth. They adored their officers and would, without hesitation, have beheaded their families if ordered to do so. Their heads were clean-shaven excepting for a tuft of long hair in the middle, by which Allah could drag them into Heaven. They used short, curiously shaped swords called Kukris with wide two cornered ends, sharp as razors, with which they artistically carved their enemies and, incidentally, shaved each other's heads. All the British officers spoke their language.

Several officers came to our house whenever possible, overjoyed at finding a friendly welcome from an English speaking family with two pretty girls. My daughter and step-daughter with her friend were invited to parties and dances at the officers' quarters and had a grand time, being fetched and brought home by their pet partners escorted always by armed Gurkhas. When we invited them to tea or a modest supper, they supplied the drinks including beer, cigarettes and most of the food. The girls made our mouths water with vivid descriptions of the wonderful dishes they had partaken of at the dances.

These suddenly ceased when the situation became more serious and there was no more time and opportunity for parties. Fighting took place on the aerodrome which changed hands several times. There were pitched battles in different parts of the town with mortars, long range guns and military planes carrying machine guns. Passenger trains, munition dumps, military convoys were ambushed and blown up, the Red Cross depot pillaged and houses occupied by Europeans set fire to. Several were burnt alive.

Women and children were shot down in the streets, sniped by natives hidden in trees. A panic started and the hospitals under military protection behind barbed wires were practically mobbed by terrified women and children who were in danger of their lives. The British troops retaliated by burning down several kampongs and arresting any armed native they came across.

Then one fine day Dikky was kidnapped. She didn't turn up for lunch and in spite of my husband's reassuring words I was anxious. I knew she had ventured out on her bicycle to see some friends so after lunch decided to walk (my bicycle having been previously stolen) to see if she were still there. At the end of the road I discovered the natives had put up a barricade and immediately surrounded me waving knives, guns and bamboo lances. They asked me what I wanted and told me to go back but, nothing daunted, I ordered them to stand aside and warned them there would be the devil to pay if anything happened to me. I was looking for my "Anak" (child) who had disappeared and was determined to find her. They consulted together and finally decided to let me pass. When I arrived at the friends' house they were having lunch and informed me Dikky had left two hours ago to return home. While we were discussing the best step to take, a native ran past and told their cook (they still had one although since some time most Europeans were without servants) my daughter had been taken with other Europeans to one of the prisons in town, the P.I.D (Private Information Department). A bicycle was lent to me and I went to see the Swiss Consular agent who at once accompanied me to town. I remained outside to guard the two bicycles and he entered the building with a British officer who was, apparently, on the same errand. To cut a long story short, all Europeans taken that morning were released, including Dikky. She told us the natives had stopped her on her way home, taken her bicycle and put her into a truck with about thirty other Europeans already arrested, and driven into town escorted by armed natives. They were still waiting to be interrogated when we arrived to demand their release, the idea being to keep them as hostages and steal the bicycles. Fortunately these were returned to their respective owners.

Another time, a young Dutch acquaintance, shortly out of camp, married to a charming French woman, and father of a small son six years old, came in to see us one morning on his way up to his family who was staying with friends. They had only been reunited since a few weeks. The same evening he was carried past our house on a stretcher to the hospital where he died at eleven pm. There had been some shooting in the vicinity and the natives, thinking he was the culprit, got hold of him and beat him to death in front of his wife. It was impossible for Europeans to defend themselves as they were not allowed to carry arms. Since already some time we were without servants, the heads of the native villages having threatened death to those who served white people, and the village ours came from, not far from our house, was particularly communistic-minded.

We were also, during several weeks, without an adequate water and gas supply. Fortunately we had a deep well in the garden and, as long as we could do so, also supplied the neighbours. Being short of water in a tropical climate is no joke. Our officer friends finally decided it would be wiser for us to leave our house and go to the part of the town included the military protection zone. So we packed what we really needed and were taken to a small hotel where we all had to do our own work and cooking. A week later we heard our house had been completely ransacked and pillaged.

One night we were told the natives intended setting fire to our hotel, so we spent the night elsewhere. However they seemed to have changed their minds and the following morning we returned. Sniping continued and Gurkhas patrolled the streets searching kampongs. Once, when standing on my balcony, a bullet wizzed past my head and lodged in the wall behind. Another day, on returning to the hotel from a foraging expedition, I found one of the officers we knew in the garden holding a Tommy gun with six natives, hands up, before him. He frightened the lives out of them, but refrained from shooting them as he told us later, they had been already disarmed by his men and he couldn't shoot an un-armed man. I confess I would not have had the same scruples. A few weeks later the same officer was sniped in the head and killed outright while searching a kampong with some Gurkhas, possibly by one of the very natives he had let off.

At Surabaya women and children being evacuated from camps by the British were blown up by natives in the trucks they were standing in, native children were throwing hand grenades.

The British themselves were, at one time, nearly pushed back into the sea.

More and more people crowded into the military protections zones and camps, where they were fed mostly on army rations. Finally when the Bandung railway station had been set on fire, the natives were ordered to the other side of town and forbidden to go beyond a certain limit. Once more it was time to move, so we left the hotel. My husband went to friends, my step-daughter and friend managed to find a furnished garage near the hospital, and Dikky and I were bound in two police cells on the outskirts of a large camp, and happy to be there although we had only two mattresses on the floor, one table and two chairs between us. We used string from one wall to another to throw our clothes over. Fortunately our cells were airy and clean. I had taken with me a small electric stove for cooking, an iron, two pans, a pail, jug and some sheets and blankets. We ate out of one plate with spoon turnabout until a kind officer took pity on us. The army kitchen provided bread, soup and tea, tinned milk and sugar, and I managed to buy some extra food such as eggs and fruit at black market prices from Chinese vendors. Here we stayed for about three weeks until we were told Swiss were being evacuated to Singapore, and there would be room for self and daughter.

We stayed in Singapore at the Swiss transit camp two months. This was the month of December 1945 until a ship taking refugees to Europe arrived.

My husband flew back six months later to Holland, and my step-daughter was able to join her husband in Borneo where he was evacuated after having been three months a super American convalescent camp in Manila.

****

During these past years I have learnt that it is impossible to judge one race by the standards of another. Many misunderstanding and troubles arise through the diversity of climate, customs, languages, habits, manner, traditions and morals.

It is not necessary to assume orientals are inhuman (what about Occindentals?) They may merely be following the way of living of their own countries and times, and can no more follow our ways of living and behaving than we theirs. The differences of peoples of this world arise from causes deep rooted in the origin of mankind, millions of years ago. Why should there necessarily be superiority or inferiority in these differences and why should one cherish the conviction that men of one's own race and kind are endowed with virtues and principles and qualities superior to those of other races and religions?

Forbearance, understanding, patience, infinite tact and tolerance alone can bridge us nearer to the ideal of Peace and Universal Brotherhood.

L. KOCH-LÜTHY
(Written between 1947 - 1960)

33

Borobudur Temple 1940 The author and Dikky

The house in Bandung

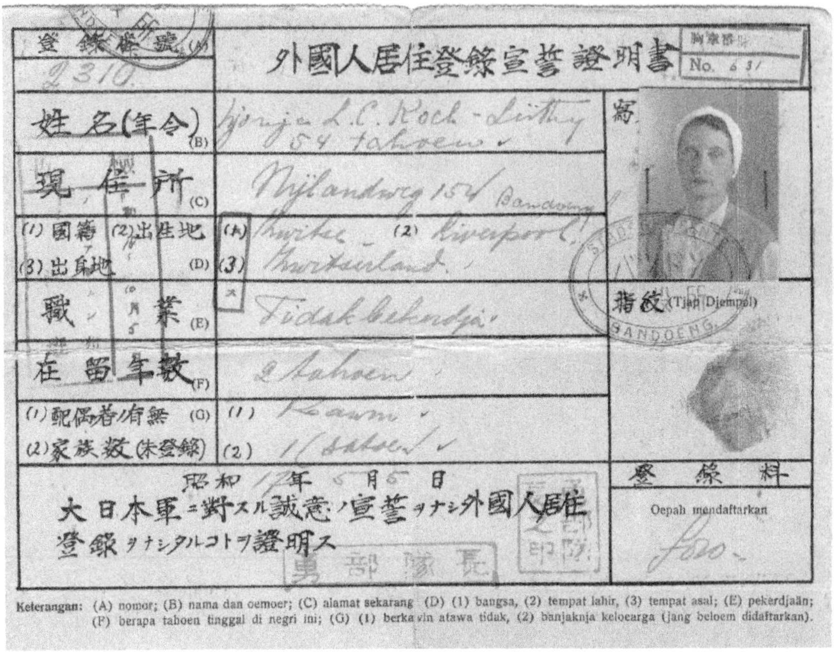

Japanese identity card with photograph and thumb print

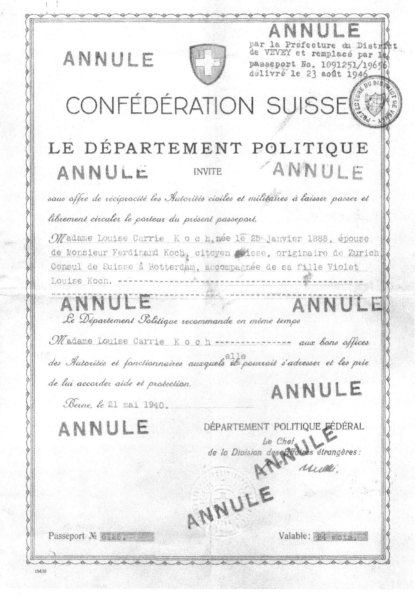

Front page of travel document for Louise Carrie Koch and her daughter Violet Louise Koch showing date of issue 21 May 1940 and return to Vevey in Switzerland 1946

Second page travel document over stamped with return journey. Stamps of Swiss consulate in Singapore and French consulate in London.

40

Third page travel document with various stamps from the flight route from Naples to Java in 1940 and stamps from return route in 1946 by sea to England and overland train to Switzerland.

Forth page travel document with various stamps from 1940 flight
route to Java and the 1946 sea route back from Java via England,
arriving in Vevey, Switzerland on 10 March 1946

Printed in Great Britain
by Amazon

25807953R00030